P9-DHZ-351

March of America Facsimile Series

Number 33

Journal of Arthur Fallows

Arthur Fallows

Journal of Arthur Fallows
by Arthur Fallows

from "Discoveries beyond the Appalachian
Mountains in September, 1671"
by David I. Bushnell, Jr.

in American Anthropologist, n s IX (1907)

ANN ARBOR

UNIVERSITY MICROFILMS, INC.

A Subsidiary of Xerox Corporation

Foreword

Unlike the French, who possessed a natural highway into the interior of North America via the St. Lawrence River and the Great Lakes, the English colonists of the 17th century confronted a formidable barrier to westward expansion by reason of the Appalachian Mountains. Curiosity to discover what lay on the other side of the mountains was keen, however. Some speculated that "the Indian Ocean" might "stretch an Arm or Bay from California into the Continent as far as the Apalataean Mountains." John Lederer, a German explorer who had come to Virginia, held this opinion and attempted three times in 1669 and 1670 to cross the mountain chain, but without success. The first successful crossing of the Appalachians of which we have any record was not accomplished until 1671. Robert Fallows (Fallam), a member of the party which performed that feat, wrote the journal reproduced here.

Abraham Wood, a prominent military leader in Virginia and a man much interested in western exploration, commissioned an expedition in 1671 for the purpose of "finding out the ebbing & flowing of the Waters on the other side of the Mountains in order to the discovery of the South Sea." A party consisting of four Englishmen and an Indian guide set out from the town of "Apomatacks" on September 1, 1671, and was later joined by more Indians whom Wood ordered to accompany them.

The journey itself was relatively uneventful as Fallows describes it except for the impressions which the mountainous terrain made on the imagination. After ascending one high mountain, Fallows remarked that "it was a pleasing tho' dreadful sight to see the mountains & Hills as if piled one upon another." Keyed up by a belief that the "South Sea" might be close at hand, one member of the party thought he saw sails in the distance, though Fallows, more accurately, thought "them to be white clifts." As they crossed over the mountains they observed that the streams now flowed in a westerly direction.

Because of difficulty in obtaining game to feed the expedition, the Indians were impatient to return. Before retracing their steps, however, the party formally claimed the territory beyond the Appalachians in the name of Charles II. After firing guns to mark the solemnity of the occasion and after carving initials on several trees as proof of their arrival, the expedition headed homeward. But when Fallows and his companions took a final look west from the top of a hill, a rising fog suggested to them the presence of a great bay. Still unsure whether the ocean was near, the party continued its march and arrived at Fort Henry, at the mouth of the James River, on October 1, two months after having begun their journey.

Two copies of Fallows' journal were made. A Dr. Daniel Coxe obtained one copy and sent it to the government in England in March of 1687. That copy is now deposited in the Public Record Office in London. The Reverend John Clayton made a second copy, presumably while he was rector at Jamestown between 1684-1686. This copy he dispatched to the Royal Society in London, before which body it was read in 1688. The Clayton copy is now among the records of the Royal Society in the British Museum. David Bushnell, who edited the Clayton copy for the *American Anthropologist*, N.S. IX (1907), has additional background information in that journal, pp. 31-56. Also useful are the notes and introduction to the same journal provided by Clarence W. Alvord and Lee Bidgood in *The First Explorations of the Trans-Allegheny Region by the Virginians, 1650-1674* (Cleveland, 1912), pp. 183-205.

DISCOVERIES BEYOND THE APPALACHIAN MOUNTAINS IN SEPTEMBER, 1671

By DAVID I. BUSHNELL, Jr

The writer has recently found in the British Museum a manuscript journal of a trip over the mountains from Virginia, made during the autumn of the year 1671. This journal is of special interest, as it is the earliest record of the crossing of the Appalachians by Europeans. The manuscript is included with many others in volume 4432, entitled " Papers Relating to the Royal Society." [1]

It is true that during the years 1669 and 1670 John Lederer made three short journeys to the westward of the then settled parts of Virginia, traveling as far as the summit of the mountains ; but it is evident he did not descend the western slope.[2] The following year, however, a party of Englishmen, with Indian guides, pushed westward until they found the waters flowing in a westerly course, showing them to have crossed the natural divide.

This expedition took formal possession of the newly discovered

---

[1] A transcript of this journal, somewhat condensed, written in the third person, and varying in many essential details from the manuscript here printed, appears in *Documents Relative to the Colonial History of the State of New York*, vol. III, pp. 193-7, New York, 1853, under the title : "The Journal & Relatior of a New Discovery made behind the Apuleian Mountains to the West of Virginia." The author of the journal is Arthur Fallows (spelled Fallam in the printed copy), a member of the expedition, as will appear by reference to the entry under date of September 14 in the two accounts, the personal pronoun being employed by the author in the original, as " Mr Fallam," in the transcript. There is a brief account of their tour in Beverley's *History of Virginia* (London, 1705, bk. I, p. 64), in which the leader of the party is called "Captain Henry Batt" ; and Mr James Mooney makes use of the journal, as printed in the New York Colonial Documents, in his *Siouan Tribes of the East* (Bulletin of the Bureau of Ethnology, Washington, 1894). In the following notes, for all of which the Editor alone is responsible, attention is called to the more important variations in the two versions by quotations from the previously printed copy. — EDITOR.

[2] *The Discoveries of John Lederer, in Three Several Marches from Virginia to the West of Carolina, and other parts of the Continent, Begun in March, 1669, and ended in September, 1670.* London, 1672 ; reprinted, Rochester, N. Y., 1902. For comments on the authenticity of parts of Lederer's narrative, see Thomas in *American Anthropologist*, V, 724-7, 1903.

lands in the name of King Charles II, as is set forth in the following journal, which is copied in full :

A JOURNAL FROM VIRGINIA, BEYOND THE APAILACHIAN MOUNTAINS, IN SEPT. 1671. SENT TO THE ROYAL SOCIETY BY Mᴿ CLAYTON, [1] AND READ AUG. 1. 1688, BEFORE THE SAID SOCIETY. —

Thomas Batts, Thomas Woods and Robert Fallows having received a commission from the honᵇˡ Major General Wood for the finding out the ebbing & flowing of the Waters on the other side of the Mountains in order to the discovery of the South Sea accompanied with *Penecute*[2] a great man of the *Apomatack* Indians[3] & Jack Weason,[4] formerly a servant to Major General Wood with five horses set forward from the Apomatacks town about eight of the clock in the morning, being Friday Sept. 1. 1671. That day we traveled above 40 miles, took up our quarters & found that we had travel'd from the *Okenechee* path due West.[5]

Sept. 2. we traveled about 45 miles and came to our quarters at Sun set & found we were to the north of the West.

Sept. 3. we traveled west and by south and about three o'clock came to a great swamp a mile and a half or two miles over and very difficult to pass. we led our horses thro' & waded twice over a River emptying itself in Roanoake River.[6] After we were over we went northwest & so came round & took up our quarters west. This day we traveled 40 miles good.

Sept. 4. We set forward and about two of the clock arriv'd at the *Sapiny* Indian Town.[7] We travelled south & by west course till about even

---

[1] See the previous communication from "The Rev. Mr John Clayton, afterwards Dean of Kildare in Ireland," on page 41.

[2] "Perecute" throughout the printed copy in the *Doc. Col. Hist. N. Y.*

[3] One of the tribes of the Powhatan confederacy of Virginia, formerly living on lower Appomatox river. Their principal village, which bore the same name and which was burned by the English in 1611, was situated on the site of Bermuda Hundred, Prince George county. In Captain John Smith's time the tribe numbered 60 warriors, or about 200 people, but it was extinct by 1722. The name signifies "river-bend" according to Gerard (*Am. Anthrop.*, VII, 223, 1905), "resting tree" according to Tooker (ibid., VI, 673, 1904).

[4] *Nesan* in the printed copy. See note 1, p. 52.

[5] "This path led from Petersburgh, Virginia, to Augusta, Georgia. It is laid down on *Mitchell's Map*, London, 1755" (*Doc. Col. Hist. N. Y.*, III, 193, note ; see also Mitchell's letter following this journal). Mooney (op. cit., pp. 35–38) locates the Occaneechi village, in 1675, at about the site of Clarksville, Mecklenburg county, southern Virginia. See Lawson, *History of Carolina*, London, 1714.

[6] Staunton river. Compare the letter of Dr John Mitchell, following.

[7] "Sapong [for Sapony] Town" in the printed copy. This village is located by Mooney (pp. 30, 35) on Otter river, southwest of Lynchburg, in Campbell county. The printed narrative continues : "They traveled S. and by W. course till about noon ", etc.

[ing] and came to the *Saponys* west.   Here we were very joyfully & kindly received with firing of guns & plenty of provisions.   We here hired a Sepiny Indian to be our gui..e towards the *Teteras*,[1] a nearer way than usual.

Sept. 5.   Just as we were ready to take horse and march from the *Sapiny's*[2] about seven of the clock in the morning we heard some guns go off from the other side of the River.   They were siven Apomatack Indians sent by Major General Wood[3] to accompany us in our Voyage. We hence sent back a horse belonging to Mr Thomas Wood, which was tired, by a Portugal, belonging to Maj. General Wood, whom we here found.[4]   About eleven of the clock we set forward and that night came to the town of the *Hanathaskies*[5] which we judge to be 25 miles from the *Sapenys*, they are lying west and by north in an Island on the *Sapony* River, rich Land.

Sept. 6.   About 11 of the clock we set forward from the *Hanathaskies*; but left Mr Thomas Wood at the town dangerously sick of the Flux, & the horse he rode on belonging to Major General Wood was likewise taken with the staggers & a failing in his hinder parts.   Our course was this day West and by South and we took up our quarters West about 20 miles from the town.[6]   This afternoon our horses stray'd away about ten of the clock.

Sept. 7.   We set forward, about three of the clock we had sight of the mountains, we travelled 25 miles over very hilly and stony Ground our course westerly.

Sept. 8.   We set out by sunrise and Travelled all day a west and by north course.   About one of the clock we came to a Tree mark'd in the

---

[1] The last two names are given respectively as "Sapong" and "Totera" in the printed copy.   The latter were the Tutelo.   See note 5, p. 48.

[2] This name is not repeated in the printed copy.

[3] Wood's name is not here mentioned in the printed copy.

[4] The printed copy reads : ". . . they were 7 Apomatock Indians sent to accompany them in their Travels, one of their horses being tired they sent him back, . . ."

[5] "Hanohaskie Indian Town" in the printed copy.   The sentence continues : "25 miles from the Sapongs, whe.e they were likewise kindly entertained, the town lyes W. and by N. in an Island of the Sapong River   Richland."   Mooney (p. 34) believes this to be a mistake for Manohaski, and identifies it with the Monahassanugh of Capt. John Smith's map, "on which they are located indefinitely southwest of the junction of the James and the Rivanna."   Mooney locates the Hanohaski (Hanathaskies) town of the present narrative on the northern ("Sapong" or "Sapinys") branch of Staunton river, in the present Bedford county, Virginia.

[6] The printed copy reads : ". . . 20 miles from the Town, this afternoon ye Indians killed them a dear, in the night 2 of their horses straied away from y^m about 10 of the clock."

past[1] with a coal M. A N I.   About four of the clock we came to the foot
of the first mountain went to the top & then came to a small descent,
& so did rise again & then till we came almost to the bottom was a very
steep descent.   We travelled all day over very stony, rocky ground and
after 30 miles travill this day we came to our quarters at the foot of the
mountains[2] due west.   We past the *Sapony* River twice this day.

Sept. 9.   We were stirring with the Sun & travelled west & after
a little riding came again to the Supany River where it was very nar-
row, & ascended the second mountain which wound up west & by
south with several springs[3] and fallings, after which we came to a steep
descent at the foot whereof was a lovely descending Valley about six
miles over with curious small risings   Our course over it
was south west.[4]   After we were over that, we came to a very steep descent, at the foot whereof stood the *Tetera*[5] Town in a very rich swamp
between a branch[6] and the main River of Roanoke circled about with
mountains.   We got thither about three of the clock after we had
travelled 25 miles.   Here we were exceedingly civilly entertain'd.

[Sept. 9–11.]   Saturday night, Sunday & monday we staid at the
Toteras.   Perceute being taken very sick of a fever & ague every afternoon, not withstanding on tuesday morning about nine of the clock we
resolved to leave our horses with the *Toteras* & set forward.

Sept. 12.   We left the town West and by North we travell'd that
day sometimes southerly, sometimes westerly as the path went[7] over
several high mountains & steep Vallies[8] crossing several branches & the

---

[1] " . . . marked in the path . . ''   The periods are omitted after the M and the
I following in the printed copy.

[2] " . . . at yᵉ foot of a Mountain . . .''

[3] "risings'' — which would seem to be the proper word.   These are the foothills of
the Blue Ridge.

[4] " . . . wᵗʰ curious small risings, sometimes indifferent good way, their course over
it was S : W : . . .''

[5] "Tolera.''   As above mentioned these were the Tutelo Indians, an eastern
Siouan tribe.   This town Mooney (op. cit., 35) locates on the headwaters of Dan river,
about the present state line, southwest of Stuart, in Patrick county, Va., or possibly
within the present limits of North Carolina.   The name Tutelo, or Totero, is a contrac-
tion of Todirich-roone, the Iroquois designation "for all the Siouan tribes of Virginia
and Carolina, including even the Catawba.''   For an excellent description of these
Indians and their final dispersion, see Mooney, pp. 37–53.

[6] "Breach.''

[7] " . . . and traveled something Southerdly, something Northerdly as the path
went, . . .''

[8] " . . . Deep descending valleys, . . .''

River Roanoke several times all exceedingly stony ground until about four of the clock *Percente* being taken with his fit and verry weary we took up our quarters by the side of Roanoke River almost at the head of it at the foot of the great mountain. Our course was west & by north, having travill'd 25 miles. At the *Teteras* we hired one of their Indians for our Guide and left one of the *Apomatock* Indians there sick.[1]

Sept. 13. In the morning we set forward early. After we had travelled about three miles we came to the foot of the great mountain & found a very steep ascent so that we could scarse keep ourselves from sliding down again. It continued for three miles with small intermissions of better way. right up by the path on the left we saw the proportions of the mon. (whereof they have given an account it seems in a former relation which I have not — Note by Mr Clayton).[2]

When we were got up to the Top of the mountain & set down very weary we saw very high mountains lying to the north & south as far as we could discern. Our course up the mountain was west by north. A very small descent on the other side and as soon as over we found the vallies tending westerly. It was a pleasing tho' dreadful sight to see the mountains & Hills as if piled one upon another. After we had travelled about three miles from the mountains, easily descending ground about 12 of the clock[3] we came to two trees mark'd with a coal MA. NI. the other cut in with MA & several other scratchments.[4]

Hard by a Run just like the swift creek at Mr Randolph's[5] in Virginia, emptying itself sometimes westerly sometimes northerly with curious meadows on each [side]. Going forward we found rich ground but having curious rising hills and brave meadows with grass about man's hight. many rivers running west-north-west and several Runs from the southerly mountains which we saw as we march'd, which run northerly into the

---

[1] This last sentence does not occur in the printed copy ; but see note 3, p. 51.

[2] The printed copy varies considerably in the wording of the entry under this date.

[3] The hour is omitted from the printed copy.

[4] ". . . wth a coale MANI ye other cut in with MA and several other Scrablem^ts hard by a pretty swift small current, tending West, sometimes Northerdly, wth curious meadows on each side, ye ground as they past was rich but stoney, pleasant riseing hills, and all along brave rich meadows, wth grass above man's hight, . ."

[5] Seemingly Henry Randolph, uncle of the celebrated Col. William Randolph who arrived in Virginia in 1674. The former settled in Virginia in 1640 and died there thirty years later. His widow married Peter Field, an ancestor of Thomas Jefferson. Colonel William Randolph established his estate on Turkey island (since disappeared) in James river, about 20 miles below Richmond. It was from this vicinity that the Batts party started on its journey.

great River.[1]   After we had travelled about 7 miles we came to a very steep descent where are found a great Run which emptied itself so we supposed into the great River northerly. our course being as the path went, west-south-west.   We set forward west and had not gone far but we met again with the River, still broad running west & by north.   We went over the great run emptying itself northerly into the great River.   After we had marched about 6 miles northwest & by north we came to the River again where it was much broader than at the two other places.   It ran here west and by south and so as we suppose round up westerly. Here we took up our quarters, after we had waded over, for the night. Due west, the soil, the farther we went [is] the richer & full of bare meadows & old fields.[2]

("Old fields" is a common expression for land that has been cultivated by the Indians & left fallow, which are generally overrun with what they call broom grass = Note by Mr Clayton)

Sept. 14.   We set forward before sunrise our provisions being all spent we travel'd as the path went sometimes westerly sometimes southerly,[3] over good ground but stony, sometimes rising hills and then steep Descents[4] as we march'd in a clear place at the top of a hill we saw lying south west a curious prospect of hills like waves raised by a gentle breese of wind rising one upon another.   Mr. Batts supposed he saw sayles: but I rather think them to be white clifts.[5]   We marched about 20 miles this day and about three of the clock we took up our quarters to see if the Indians could kill us some Deer. being west & by north, very weary and hungry & Perceute continued very ill yet desired to go forward.   We came this day over several brave runs and hope tomorrow to see the main River again.[6]

Sept. 15.   Yesterday in the afternoon and this day we lived a Dog's life—hunger & ease.   Our Indians having done their best could kill us

---

[1] The editor of the *N. Y. Doc. Col. Hist.* in a note identifies this with the "Great Kanhawa," but it is really New river, its chief tributary from the southeast.

[2] ". . . and so as they suppose tended W : here they took up their quarters, after they had waded over the soyle, the further they past the richer, and stony, full of brave meadows and old feilds, the course W."

[3] ". . . sometimes Southerdly, sometimes Northerdly . . ."

[4] ". . . steep descending valleys . . ."

[5] ". . . riseing one behind another,   Mr Batts supposed he saw houses, but Mr Fallam rather tooke them to be white cliffs."

[6] The printed entry for this date ends: " · · · they past this day several brave brookes or small Rivelets."

no meat.   The Deer they said were in such herds and the ground so dry
that one or other of them could spy them.[1] About one of the clock we
set forward & went about 15 miles over some exceedingly good, some indifferent[2] ground, a west and by north course till we came to a great run
that empties itself west and by north as we suppose into the great River
which we hope is nigh at hand.   As we march'd we met with some wild
gooseberries and exceeding large haws with which we were forced to feed
ourselves.[3]

Sept. 16. Our guides went from us yesterday & we saw him no more
till we returned to the *Toras*.[4] Our Indians went aranging betimes
to see & kill us some Deer or meat.   One came and told us they heard
a Drum & a Gun go off to the northwards.   They brought us some exceedingly good Grapes & killed two turkies which were very welcome and
with which we feasted ourselves and about ten of the clock set forward &
after we had travelled about 10 miles one of our Indians killed us a Deer &
presently afterwards we had sight of a curious River like Apamatack
River.[5] Its course here was north and so as we suppose runs west about
certain curious[6] mountains we saw westward. Here we had up our quarters,
our course having been west.[7] We understand the *Mohecan* Indians did
here formerly live.   It cannot be long since for we found corn stalks in
the ground."[8]

Sept. 17. Early in the morning we went to seek some trees to mark
our Indians being impatient of longer stay by reason it was like to be bad
weather, & that it was so difficult to get provisions. We found four trees
exceeding fit for our purpose that had been half bared[9] by our Indians,

---

[1] ". . . The Dear they said were in such heards, and the ground drye, yᵗ by the
rattleing of the leaves they easely espied yᵐ. . . ."

[2] "stony" for "indifferent."

[3] ". . . wᵗʰ wᶜʰ they were forced to fill themselves, feeding on these and yᵉ hopes
of better success on the morrow.   They had hired an Indian guide from the Tolera who
goeing to kill yᵐ some dear lost them."   Compare note 1, p. 49.

[4] This opening sentence is combined with the closing sentence of the printed trans-
script.   See the last note.

[5] ". . . they had a sight of a curious River like the Thames agᵗ Chelcey, but had a
fall yᵗ made a great noise whose course was there N. . . ."   In a footnote Jefferson is
cited as identifying this fall with "the Great falls of the Kanhawa, 90 miles above the
mouth."

[6] ". . . certain pleasant mountains, . . ."

[7] ". . . here they took up their quarters, and found their course had been W. and
by N."

[8] The last sentence of this entry in the printed copy reads : "Here they found Indian Feilds wᵗʰ corne stalks in them, and understood afterward the Mohetans had lived
there not long before " . . .

[9] ". . . bark'd . . "

standing after one the other.   We first proclaimed the King in these words :
" Long live Charles the Second, by the grace of God King of England,
Scotland, France, Ireland & Virginia & of all the Territories thereunto
belonging.   Defender of the faith etc." firing some guns and went to the
first tree which we marked thus, ⚓ with a pair of marking irons for
his sacred majesty.

Then the next thus **WB** for the right honb^le Governor Sir William
Berkley, the third thus : **AW** for the honble. Major General Wood.
The last thus : **ℬ** : R F · P. for Perceute who said he would learn
Englishman. & on another tree hard by stand these letters one under
another   T T . N. P. V E. R [1] after we had done we went ourselves
down to the river side ; but not without great difficulty it being a piece
of very rich ground where on the Moketans [2] had formerly lived, & grown
up with weeds & small prickly Locusts & Thistles [3] to a very great height
that it was almost impossible to pass.   It cost us hard labour to get thro !
When we came to the River side we found it better and broader than expected, much like James River at Col. Stagg's, the falls much like these
falls.   We imagined by the Water marks it flows here about three feat. [4]
It was ebbing Water when we were here.   We set up a stick by the
Water side but found it ebb very slowly.   Our Indians kept such a
hollowing that we durst not stay any longer to make further tryal. [5]   Immediately upon coming to our quarters we returned homewards and when
we were on the top of a Hill we turned about & saw over against us,
westerly, over a certain delightful hill a fog arise and a glimmering light

---

[1] In the printed copy the inscriptions following that for King Charles are : " **W B**
for the Governor Sir William Berkley, the 3d Tree w^th **AW** for the Major General
Abraham Wood the last tree thus **TⷣℬH** for themselves " — a rather senseless com-
bination for Abraham Wood and Robert Fallows.   Then follows the paragraph : " P
for Perecute who said he would be an English man "   Then another paragraph : "And on
another Tree stands these letters for ye rest one under another [¶] **I N.** [for Jack
Nesan, or Weason,] **T T. N P. V. E R.**"   Thomas Woods, or Wood, was left behind
with the Hanahaskies on September 6 (see also entry of September 21), hence his initials
do not appear.   What names the remaining initials represent are not known.

[2] " Mohetons " in the printed copy.

[3] From the word "thistles" to the end of the next sentence ("get thro !") does
not appear in the printed copy.

[4] . . . The printed copy differs so radically as to suggest that a part of the present
manuscript had been omitted ; but this is not the case.   The former reads : . . . "better
and broader than expected, full as broad as the Thames over ag^t Waping, ye falls, much
like the Falls of James River in Virginia, and imagined by the Water Marks it flowed there
about 3 foot."

[5] " . . . further tryall least they should leave y^m ".

as from water. We supposed there to be a great Bay.[1] We came to the
Toteras[2] Tuesday night where we found our horses, and ourselves wel
entertain'd. We immediately had the news of M[r] Byrd & his great
company's Discoveries three miles from the *Tetera's* Town. We have
found *Mohetan* Indians who having intelligence of our coming were afraid
it had been to fight them and had sent him to the *Totera's* to inquire.
We gave him satisfaction to the contrary & that we came as friends, pre-
sented him with three or four shots of powder. He told us by our
Interpreter, that we had [been] from the mountains half way to the place
they now live at. That the next town beyond them lived upon plain
level, from whence came abundance of salt.[3] That he could inform us no
further by reason that there were a great company of Indians that lived
upon the great Water.[4]

Sept 21. After very civil entertainment we came from the *Toteras*
& on Sunday morning the 24th we came to the *Hanahaskies*. We found
M[r] Wood dead & burried & his horse likewise dead. After civil entertainment, with firing of guns at parting which is more than usual.

Sept. 25 on monday morning we came from thence & reached to
the *Sapony's* that night where we stayed till wednesday.

Sept. 27 We came from thence they having been very courteous to
us. At night we came to the *Apamatack*[5] Town, hungry, wet & weary.

Oct 1 being Sunday morning we arrived at Fort Henry.[6] God's
holy name be praised for our preservation. [7]

---

[1] The verbiage varies greatly in the print, but the principal change is " Bog " for
Bay. Compare the Clayton letter, following.

[2] " Toleras,'' as usual.

[3] Regarded by Mooney (op. cit., p. 36) as " probably about the present Mercer Salt
Works on New river, in Summers county, West Virginia, or Salt pond in the adjacent
Giles county, Virginia, so that the Mohetan must have lived within the mountains at the
head of the New river on the western border of Virginia.''

[4] The preceding entry is considerably condensed in the printed copy, and no reference is made to " M[r] Byrd and his great company's Discoveries.'' This individual
should not be confounded with the celebrated Col. William Byrd, who did not come to
America until 1674 — three years after the present expedition was made. See the Clayton letter, following.

[5] " Apomatocks town.'' " Hungry, wet & weary '' does not appear in the print. The
entries from September 21 to October 1, inclusive, are condensed in seven lines under
the single date " Sep[br] 21st.''

[6] Fort Henry was built by Lord Delawarr, in 1610, at or near Kiequotank, now
Hampton, at the mouth of James river.

[7] " Christo duce et auspice Christo.''